Talk to eyes, body and silence

Business is all about talking

Take the talk

Ferry Dawson

Talking is listening

- First half of talking is listening to others like sacrifice, and taking notice of business customers to work on everything to get across them by saying, recording and informing without any hesitation so that we can criticise our work and words without any judgement of business stakeholders.

Talk by eyes

- Truthful communication with customers can easily find you by the way of making your eye contact with smile, trouble, secrets, confidence, winner attitude, concern, controlled attention and strength of making your customers happy with business culture instead of your self.

Talk by feelings

- The most powerful and difficult yet effective manner is strictly accepting through pangs of hard dense feelings of business stakeholders that you have to convert Business into future useful asset of Customer as your quick, lazy, angry, unclear, happy or excited about the right and wrong for the family.

Talk in gestures

- Take body language workshop and Customer must be cared for and not scared of business interaction with interruption of Customer emotions like that slap in arm or squinted eye to Business and goals explanation of intended balance but not without interest of customer needs.

Business talks

- Professional talking and thinking are not same as that goes along arrow without stopping nor coming back to your bow of mouth unless of other's repartees then to get your entry to new and exciting or unpleasant thought that precedes reason for disruption of Customer experience to delight or issues.

Talk Business

- Don't worry about people who consider them selves to be king rather than kind
- Spare others of your non business details
- Space your self away from talking about complex and simple personal life but only private to others
- Mention the right facts of business and Customer need to person in name only.

Talk Businesses

- Talk groups, talk games and talk building trust should be trained in alternate experiments with customers and employee to get new understanding of mistakes and surprise gift for novel benchmark transition mechanism to be looked at as a business touch with your talking after achievements and not reverse.

Talk soon

- Snappy answers can get better attention that brings default trust and commercial contributions together to get your weaknesses unearthed, make inroads into future solutions and deflate false confidence in our little talks that arise out of strategic thinking about complex and esoteric issues.

Talk instead

- I need to remain passionate about you as listener of business things to prove your thoughts right by satisfying Customer ears, sometimes it takes time and challenge with consideration but has to be said by you what Customers want to hear.

Talk later

- Give gaps that are talking about complex situations where your mouth or other forms of communication can grow hurdles in business administration and not let anyone focus on main course of Customer goal process and attainment activities.

Talk by silence

- Understand that space in silence of Customer as your need for self-sanitizing and acceptance of business criticism or other forms of indecent exposure of business with globalisation in the lengthy process of establishing, learning and growing while interacting and knowing what you think in silence.

Talk in person

- Visit and invite the stakeholders in business contexts of common interest, commercial contributions, change continuity and not bothered to spare a point or exaggerate facts or urge arguments where your business needs more presence and not chatter.

Talk to empower

- Talking gives you access to power and sense of esteem to open Customer to competitors of direct comparison, and that alone gives scope of strategic innovation but not without any risk of getting worded or misworded.

Talk to communicate

- Convert the right kind of actions reaching Customer and Business etiquette to negotiate and close with customers from complaints to complement to get the cause championed instead of rubbing on the wrong side.

Talk in letter

- Don't delay in writing by all sincere apologies and commitment including thanks because we humans as Customer, and other stakeholders tend to secretly enjoy your self depreciation and amortization of business goals to succumb to checks of Customer.

Talk in phone

- Greet the customer
- Listen to stakeholders
- Response should be given timely, respectfully and not something of rehearsed but genuine
- Treat yourself as being present in front of the phone caller and not one of many invisible reps.

Talk in work

- Work talks
- Talk by action and change your business credibility to boost your relationship
- Talk in customer jargon and teach others mediation in customer language
- Show all proof of business changes, efforts, results and not the same for all talking.

Talk about ethics

- Remind your seniors, peers, subordinates, bosses, novices and others about expertise, trust, confidence, time and risk as the major global silent causes no easy to invest and return before you attain irrelevant complaints or retrieve good wishes of Customer as your business is paralyzed otherwise.

Talk again

- Real business challenges and importances lie in laying the right amount of emphasis on the right kind of actions reaching people who are innovative and informative but not to pay attention to detail and above all talking itself
- They work sincerely but you have to repeat the key points that go into future ideation and learning by intuition instead of rote and experience.

Talk against

- Don't worry about the right Business and personal answers of employees, Customer, and stakeholders in the global habits of tasks, thought and time to enjoy, explain or save on talking to just focus on completion for Customer praise and market progression as preparation for leadership or satisfaction of stakeholders.

Talk products

- Talk to create understanding of business products to berate the competitors and customers are not unaware of the true and false confidence in the talk
- Talk to simplify the productization and not to get the complex business jargon across your customers

Talk process improvement

- Talk to management and leadership of overcoming the challenges of physical business operations via products or end-user success
- Tell about the consistent journey of technology implementation and its new improvement in different processes

Talk ideas, not people

- The constant and continuity of business but not people who are changing resources entails to discuss with others nothing but for ideas on improving customer experience and personality
- Telling your ideas should probably open up new ways of reusing technology but people are vulnerable to tussles and differences so better not talk about others
others weaknesses.

Mistakes and mistalks

- Mistakes ought to be accepted, discussed, and not escaped from Customer attention to earn default resolution because you can't ignore something that a customer is concerned with
- Talking personal, uncomfortable and irrelevant topics can take you out of business with unusual Customer repugnance.

Talk quality

- Talk development and decent language but not four letter words in adjustments to mistakes or exaggerated sale pitch to cover Business and personal flaws.
- Talk to show how much effort was put to work for quality and how good quality resulted in the output as it is or comparison of competition.

Talk questions

- Take questions posed by competitors, Customer, employees and stakeholders in the right stead, to get new shoes responding with the pose for similar leader, producer, boss, and Business representative
- Pose questions and suggestions that you see others thinking, discovering, and accepting the right, unknown and new things.

Talk jargon

- Customised jargon pertinent to Business offerings and Customer must be quick output of research and practice of business changes, application of business skills and relevant knowledge that count in ringing technical excellence.
- Don't use jargon in interaction needing your language.

Talk resources

- Talk to machine with the care and method of correctly using it
- Talk to men with instinct to enable them but not disappoint to get best efforts and results
- Talk to materials with quality of business changes to save, consume, modify or invest

Hire speakers

- Train employees and stakeholders in business etiquette and ways of talking
- Adaptation to personal ways is better than adherence to universal formula for communication with speech, writing, behaviour, response, action, gesture or other forms of voiced and non talks.

Talk in preparation

- Spare your self to a real-time speech but prepare for the talk however informal and trivial it may be
- Rehearsal and self talking about complex and simple topic can grow trained user and inspiring conversation for future others.

Talk in place

- Talk in the context of business time and not big hot arguments to satisfy self and every one to sell your errors to customers who can desert you for want of genuine Business providers in all uncertainty of business markets and trends in guarantee to Innovation strategies.

Talk loud and soft

- To connect with new customer
- To induct new business stakeholders
- To get new ideas on acceptance
- To instill listeners intent in ignorant people
- To get a message across

Talk timely

- To ensure intelligent solutions
- To enable solutions getting acted upon by employees
- To avoid extreme trespassing on past failure and unseen future Sandcastle
- To impress market and communication-hungry

Talk to some

- Don't worry about people to do overtalking
- Be silent with some implied talkative and not bothered to spare ears
- Talk to few other to learn and adapt or practice and teach
- Talk to important but decision savvy.

Talk harsh and clear

- When errors and incompletion hinder progress of team, performance of products and people obstruct Customer acceptance or satisfaction in the end
- Be clear in your expectations and methods of business implementation warning for failure consequences and dereliction of duties.

Talk fast and hard

- When others behave unreasonable and irrational to be stubborn and unacceptably of your right way to get new chance of getting them profitable lest they should switch to Business rivals or vengeance or narrow minded focus on unnecessary things.

Talk slow and recent

- What is unimportant and not relevant to market gets passed by. Talk in slow when you get to make a point to large audience to tell latest knowledge and public cause bringing together caution and corrections to act upon for consideration with acceptance.

Talk options

- We are well aware of everybody's states of mind before reacting and interpreting to get possible or ruining on the discussed opportunity so much that you have to be looking for new business alternative without wasting time and talk
- At times we act as unaware of the other stakeholders' instincts being caught in awkward and funny prejudices, emotions and thoughts.

Talk Etiquette

- Talk in work terms of please, and thank you for creating future business growth
- Say hello and good luck with your heart and smile
- Say sorry without worry
- Your behaviour should enable warmth, willingness and interaction with customers now and later but not reluctance.

More than 80% chalk dust
MEETING TALK

Talk notes

- Prepare for the duration and topics to discuss broadly and briefly
- Leave some space for spontaneous talk
- Take note of the other side as new and unknown topic is brought up
- Be good learner always

Open with nonchalant talk

- Don't jump to get your entry to dominate or conclude your goals first
- Let it be warm shake and informal beginning whether Customer or competition or market participants
- Let the other side drive but you have to ensure that key points are not skipped

Fill in your points

- Take cues from your talker, gather thought, present information to get them going in your direction without ever missing their mouthful of words sensible or bullshit but clarifying the doubts and not bothered to controlling or exaggerating any of business effort

Be considerate of others points

- Agree with others strong points
- Accept your mistakes
- Describe the other's fault
- Leverage the right kind of thought and leave the easy way out

Talk in moderation

- Listen more than judgement
- Note more than nitpicking
- Talk more deeply than words or time
- Try to make point by allowing it to be understood by others

Conclude it

- For your points you are sure to repeat important action points with your new inputs
- For others if you conclude by stressing the attached dependency with your appreciation it is easy to bear fruitful and useful discussion to be used in future discussion

Circulation of business minutes

- Inform others whether directly or not relevant to be learners and critics of business decisions, individual failure and not hiding your department progress through business changes to save time with future evolution of business

Talk action points next time

- Elaborate on what needs to be done
- Spare what would be done for your next meeting
- Zero in on the understanding that is supposed to be right and full
- Don't worry about reaching the end of the discussion in every meeting

Appreciate others talks

- Quote others
- Reference to the different types of ideas and actions should not deviate but enrich your business credibility and Customer need not be worried about you not having enough focus or food for action

Oppose free talk

- Don't you become a member of friend in adjustments in the variety of business talking to address full range of topics
- Don't let others annoy and enjoy their ego satisfaction by allowing reactions of snobbish, cultural and religious fervor to be cool contenders for business debates

Meeting talk

- The aim is to convert doubt into understanding
- The goal is not just consensus on the right and wrong but some middle ground for Customer to meet with her needs and your capabilities
- The recognition is no longer being considered for healthy voice but healthy understanding of Customer

Winning

- Business talking is listening to get your customer win but not to becoming the best speaker yourself
- If you appreciate Customers instead of your reps that goes along winning future participation of Customer without whom all talking can grow weeds.

Talk like Ceaser

- Say sharply and precisely
- Don't worry about words threatening others
- Be fine sounding like that whistle of alarm
- Inform good and bad but not without any cost or effects

Listen like Napoleon

- Make mental maps
- Adjustments to tactical Strategy could be managed by discussion further on each new thread and facet of business participants in talking
- Try to get feedback from non talkers in person
- Try to make space for stupid talkers to get innovative solutions

Entertain like Shakespeare

- Talk in eye contact with confidence and control on your speech and words
- Use right language but adapt to get understanding of Customer
- Including atleast one Customer in your business talk can save money and time for future.

Justify like Picasso

- Depending on your next activities with knowledge that explains why and how to overcome critical juncture and facilitate the success of your customers on different colours, clear outline but abstraction of Customer ideas
- Draw your picture to draw Customer attention to detail on what you would sell.

Read like book

- Become a talking book to be knower of business and Customer facts, statistics, limitations and updates from books
- Be informed whether you attend or not about complex issues brought out from meeting
- Remember to improve yourself for later whether you're appreciated or criticised by others

Tracking and talking

- What you talk should be after you think and for listener to think big after your talking
- Try to align with others
- Don't take big deviation
- Don't worry about addressing all points covered by all

Giving and taking time

- Give others to talk about 3-5 minutes each time for not more than 5 times in each meeting of 5-10 people who are sharing and noting information
- Talk by taking time out of moderation to address, respond, and reinvent your business talk about your and other topics

Talk without stopping

- Don't take longer pause for your listeners to nod, note or tag you in Facebook or LinkedIn
- Don't tell tales and stories to entertain to prove your worth as talker
- Talk once and keep quiet if you don't see yourself as value addition

Utilising special speaking talent

- Some people have a knack for problem solving and not a customer insinuation could deviate them from Customer as star Business goal
- Coaching speaking out against lies and not bothered by how truth treats them profitable employees can grow to loyalty of Customer and other stakeholders.

Tense speaking

- First gathering facts, relevant information about people, and complex issues of opportunity can get better attention to dialogue and Customer is audience to new perspective on each combination of positive and negative sides of business

Soft whispers

- It's a habit of struggling speaker to talk in whisper on abnormal softness but it should never shatter confidence of Customer and participants including you
- Is better to talk in sturdy voice and steady firm tone

No to hiccup

- Drink water but not the risk of misunderstanding and irksome listener generated by you
- Let others take over the talk while you have a breather to waters
- Offer water if someone is not able to make it through hiccups

Chattering talks

- Do anything to stop subtalks to be single speaker at a time
- Don't answer topics overheard but directly brought up
- Avoid shouting to be heard

Overheated talks

- Identify reason that boosts ego and crush ego unless they are Customers because it's their hard-earned money
- Don't worry about winning the discussion or proving right and wrong

Shy listeners

- Open up your ears
- Don't neglect appreciation, criticism and advice
- You can talk better only if you listen better without many nods and interruptions of questions and suggestions that should come only when asked

Talk true
SOME ERRANDS

False hopes

- Don't go to release people into deluge of dreams by your speech
- You can be owner of hopes but don't tell Customer to hope for miracles
- Don't raise hope if you could not fulfill the same

Bloated claims

- Speakers adjusting with text or wordings to sail Customer in bloating glory of company against competitors could not escape reality for long to misguide Customer to wrong knowledge and reason to trust your business.

Control promise s

- Don't promise one thing a day and deliver nothing
- Control your words in dignity
- Ask what Customer wants if only you can give othwise give and ask what more they want

Constant bragging

- The goal is not a big bang busting methods of promoting, boasting, declaration or exaggerated claims to efforts, essentially means that you have to say that your products cannot support, do or say on your behalf

Teary emotions

- Don't cry in emotions
- Don't confuse Customer
- Don't force Customer
- Don't cheat Customer
- Don't forget your customer is also a human being.

Fiery affirmation

- Some people have a habit of throwing fiery and ferocious statement and that fizzles to poor quality and weak sorts of things that matter least to market, competitors and users
- Stay behind such pulls and avoid extreme financial commitments to wasted efforts.

Customer is many

- Customer is able to get new clients
- Customer is answer to your many questions
- Customer is key to Business lockouts
- Customer is many- in- one

Single Customer

- Single Customer is as important as a business per se
- Single Customer could close or open new opportunity
- Single Customer is beginning of the world of loyalty and success of your business credibility.

One Customer represents a family

- One Customer buys on behalf of her family
- She is interface between the different products and preferences of sellers and users
- She buys from one seller for multiple consumers at home or office
- She is welcome influence on the friend community.

Circles of Customer

- The customer affinities lie in kin, friends, family, extended family and professional network circles some of which emerge as the customer involves in new ideas and actions, so Companies need to work with many mays

Business circle

- The business comprises of Customer in the core, and employees, investors, stakeholders, partners, suppliers, at every peripheral and external perimeter to provide protection, simple guidelines, various services, innovative products and alternative opportunities to customers.

Array your dreams

- Tell Customers how your technologies can grow Customer dreams into future modern solutions and product innovation for Customer by taking time to allow Customer dreams to be your own otherwise could offer your business ideas for selling needs and dreams to customers.

Talk not

- When you reach your goals let them do the talking about you and you should bear silence to get new ideas on investing in customer power creation of future business changes suggested by Customer to be looked as leaders of Customer.

Accompanying Customer

- Talk to empower Customer with confidence and courage
- Talk when Customer needs you
- Talk when Customer is alone but not happy
- Talk to let the customer be heard

Always supporting Customer

- Praise the right attitude and help customers achieve improvement on results
- Don't scare the customer in any way
- Hear out but don't jump to judgement
- Tolerance and respect are foundation for Customer trust.

Trust building

- Mettle of business lies in building trust in customer segments
- Interaction, acceptance, amendment, error correction, and not anger are giving more space to customer for true worth discovery and reliance upon company for new needs satisfaction.

Have big nose

- Cut the nose where anger rubs in
- There's a lot of people who consider coming to your talking to just cut your nose by insults
- Smell the different types of rats in different directions to avoid extreme reactions

Don't compete

- Don't measure the number of words spoken by others
- Don't worry if you spoke once and sense
- Don't talk to empower your voicy victory over Customer and Business stakeholders
- Don't worry if others want you to shut-up.

If others word you

- The other side may want you not to say but listen and enjoy their skill. Discover their smartness and communication if someone voices your ideas and thoughts. We will think alike. Keep quiet until the next good reason for talking comes to you rather than discussing vaguely.

Talk to be understood

- Talk to empower your audience and not to open up your business jargon. If it involves others ignoring you, then silence is better than being slighted and misunderstood. Wait for the opportune time and mode of communication however later it may be.

Talk is communication but not

- Talk is cheap
- Talk is sweet
- Talk is hostile
- Talk may be a means to understand you but not a big deal with reward or punitive effects.

Silence is myth

- Silence is deafening
- I'll be considered as ghost if I don't talk
- Silence increases your retention power and reduces fear of personal limitations
- Silence is not respected for the same reasons as that of narrow mindset
- Silence remains gold.

Free your mind not mouth

- It is hard to keep your mouth closed but some effort should be given to free your mind from blind belief and narrow competitive knowledge.
- Don't feel that speech will go to free your mind from Customer worries. Understand Customer and talk building trust in customer.

Tie words not thought

- Let Customer think freely and help customers to voice their inner aspirations by tying words to image or action in support of business abilities to be translators of Customer dreams to reality unless they have a competitor service to your business abatement.

Control your words, not joy

- Let happiness light up your face by smile
- Don't let word reveal your joy
- Words should be counted but not joy
- Word will continue to go irreversible like a free arrow out of bow
- Joy cannot be misunderstood.

Control your mind to trust your mouth

- The serene mind need not weigh words nor prepare for communication because anyway you have controlled mind strengthening your control on communication by default and not by studying books on the same. Trust and self-confidence build up with your mind in the path.

Mind vs body language

- Mind governs the body and vice versa. A thief will think wild. A mind reader will continue to find consensus points for Customer. The business should try to train employees and customers to refine the communication with mindfulness.

Mind language

- The perception, and interpretation of business stakeholders would not be visible to customers but in simple decision making, complaints handling, products and services
- Before that you are prone to disclose understanding in your speech and communication. So try to think good.

Body movements

- Body language is needed beyond English or other forms of voice and written communication
- Eyes should be smiling, interacting and moving while talking to more than two
- Leg should walk around and not kicking podium nor scaring listener nor distracting them.
- Waist, thighs, thoracic region including spine should be straight not swinging.

Mean business

- Meaningful conversations about buying preferences are better than discussing your children or spouses and parents. The impact is not denied but emotional forcing is not good for business prospects when buyers come back to senses after leaving your talk.

Don't let

- Listener shut down mind from your talking. Ask questions. Face sarcastic remarks. Don't let assumptions dust your value. Allow listener interrupt your business speech. End soon..

www.ingramcontent.com/pod-product-compliance
Lightning Source LLC
Chambersburg PA
CBHW020552220526
45463CB00006B/2279